DATE DUE 12/16

			PRINTED IN U.S.A.

D0859268

SURVIVING
FAMILY VIOLENCE

**DELILAH BANKS AND
JOHN GIACOBELLO**

rosen publishing's
rosen
central®

NEW YORK

This book is dedicated to all survivors of domestic violence.

Published in 2016 by The Rosen Publishing Group, Inc.
29 East 21st Street, New York, NY 10010

Library of Congress Cataloging-in-Publication Data

Banks, Delilah.
  Surviving family violence / Delilah Banks and John Giacobello.
      pages cm. – (Family issues and you)
  Includes index.
  ISBN 978-1-4994-3707-2 (library bound) – ISBN 978-1-4994-3705-8 (pbk.) – ISBN 978-1-4994-3706-5 (6-pack)
  1. Family violence–Juvenile literature. 2. Family violence–Prevention–Juvenile literature. I. Giacobello, John. II. Title.
  HV6626.B274 2016
  613.6'6–dc23
                                                                                    2015016288

Manufactured in the United States of America

CONTENTS

INTRODUCTION

You've probably heard of family violence before, but may not know exactly what it is or the ways it affects you. There are several names people use to refer to violence at home: domestic violence, family violence, spousal abuse, and child abuse are the most common. Unfortunately, many of you reading this may have witnessed different kinds of violence at home. And even if you haven't, chances are that somebody that you know—either at school, in your neighborhood, or on a sports team or in a club with you—has. Family violence is an issue that affects everybody. By understanding what it means, its warning signs, and how to stop it, anybody can become an ally in the fight to end family violence.

The U.S. Department of Justice (DOJ) defines family violence as "all types of violent crime committed by an offender who is related to the victim either biologically or legally through marriage or adoption." In a narrower sense, some people use the term "domestic violence" to refer to violence between spouses or domestic partners. For our purposes, family or domestic violence will include child abuse and elder abuse as well.

There are a lot of myths about family violence. Some people think it is only physical. Many people also think that only men commit violence against women and children. These aren't true. The DOJ clarifies that family

Violence at home can be worrisome. Whether you're a victim of abuse or you witness abuse between parents or other family members at home, don't feel helpless. There are ways to stop family violence.

violence can be "physical, sexual, emotional, economic, or psychological." And just like men, women also commit family violence, and men can be victims, too. Furthermore, members of the LGBTQ (lesbian, gay, bisexual, transgender, and queer) community also face violence from partners or parents. By debunking the myths and understanding how to stop family violence, you can help your own family or a friend end an abusive situation at home.

CHAPTER ONE

WHAT IS FAMILY VIOLENCE?

Violence in families is one of the biggest problems facing our society today. In 2012, data collected nationwide by the Federal Bureau of Investigation (FBI) indicated over five hundred thousand reported offenses between family members. Unfortunately, this statistic doesn't account for all those victims who did not or could not safely report violence in their homes.

Whenever violence happens between members of a family, it is considered to be family violence. Another common term you may hear is "domestic violence." Whichever name is used to refer to it, know that violence at home is never okay.

RECOGNIZING ABUSE

You have probably already seen a TV show or heard a news story about an abused, or battered, wife. Maybe a teacher has talked to your class about child abuse. Perhaps you were at a friend's house and didn't like the way his or her elderly grandparent was being treated. These things may have made you wonder about your own family.

How do you know if you are being abused? If your mom, dad, or any other family member has ever hit you, does that mean you are an abused child? Unfortunately, the answer is not simple. For instance, most people wouldn't call a light smack on the bottom for swiping a cookie before dinner "family violence." But if that smack came from a heavy stick or if it were a punch hard enough to leave a bruise, many people would consider it abuse.

Some parents may have different opinions about whether or not it is okay to spank their kids in order to teach them right from wrong, but no parent has the right to beat or bruise another family member. When a parent does this, it is not for the good of the child. Violence is never an act of love.

Unlike violence, true discipline is an act of love. It is done to teach children lessons about life. But discipline and abuse are two different things. Think of the example of a teenage daughter who stays out past curfew. Most parents would be upset if their daughter came home an hour after curfew. They might be worried about teaching her to be responsible or worried about her safety. In order to discipline their daughter, these parents might ground her or assign extra chores.

There is a fine line between discipline and violence. All parents should discipline their children and teach them lessons about life, but verbal or physical abuse is never acceptable.

While this punishment might feel unfair for the daughter, deep down she would probably still understand that her parents love her. If your parents have ever disciplined you, you probably knew deep down that your parents were trying to teach you an important lesson, even if you thought their actions were unfair.

But when parents use violence to teach their child a lesson, it is no longer discipline. Violence is hurtful, and it is abuse.

WHAT ARE THE DIFFERENT KINDS OF ABUSE?

Some people think that abuse can only be physical. But abuse can also be directed toward a person's mind or emotional well-being. Physical actions such as hitting, beating, and kicking are called physical abuse. They are considered physical because they harm the body. Abuse against a person's mind or well-being, such as persistent, nasty teasing or prolonged, uncontrolled yelling or screaming, is called emotional abuse. Emotional abuse is less outwardly visible.

Some people think abuse is only physical, but emotional abuse—such as yelling, screaming, or cruel teasing—can be just as scarring to a person's well-being.

Family members are supposed to try to help each other feel good about themselves. But when they abuse one another emotionally, they use words that harm rather than help. Being abused in this way can make a person feel worthless. Hurtful words are especially bad for younger kids, because they almost always believe what they are told. If a child is told that he or she is useless or stupid, that belief may stay with him or her into adulthood. Of course, adults can be hurt by words, too.

Another kind of abuse is neglect. This is when family members' basic needs are not met. A parent may not provide his or her children or spouse with food, clothing, or shelter. A parent may simply ignore his or her children or spouse. Love and attention are also basic needs.

Elder abuse is a commonly under-recognized form of neglect. Because elderly grandparents who live with their families often cannot take care of their own needs, they are dependent upon their children or grandchildren to take care of them. When their basic needs are ignored, it is considered abuse.

Sexual abuse is another type of family violence that is unfortunately common. Sexual abuse occurs when one family member forces another to engage in undesired sexual activity or touches the person in ways that he or she does not want to be touched. Because no child under the age of consent (usually either sixteen or eighteen years old in most states) has the legally recognized ability to agree to sexual activity, sexual activity with an underage family member is always abuse, regardless of whether or not that child claims to have agreed to or wanted to engage in a sexual act.

LGBTQ VICTIMS OF FAMILY VIOLENCE

Most people generally think of domestic violence as a crime committed by heterosexual men against their wives and children. However, this stereotype is harmful to one significant population of victims of family violence: members of the LGBTQ community.

As noted in a September 2014 article in *Advocate*, "the National Violence Against Women Survey [which was sponsored in 1996 by the National Institute of Justice (NIJ), the National Center for Injury Prevention and Control (NCIPC), and the Centers for Disease Control and Prevention (CDC)] found that 21.5 percent of men and 35.4 percent of women living with a same-sex partner experienced intimate-partner physical violence in their lifetimes." The same survey also noted a 34.6 percent incidence rate among transgender respondents.

In 2010, the CDC carried out the National Intimate Partner and Sexual Violence Survey, in which the rates were found to have risen even higher among these populations. Reports of physical violence, rape, and stalking rose to 43.8 percent among lesbian respondents and 26 percent among gay men. While domestic violence in LGBTQ relationships often shares many of the same characteristics as abuse in heterosexual, cisgender relationships, LGBTQ victims of domestic violence face the added threat of being "outed" to coworkers or family members and the risk of being mistreated or ignored by police. A 2010 survey by the National Coalition of

(continued on the next page)

(continued from the previous page)

Anti-Violence Programs found that 45 percent of LGBTQ victims are denied services at domestic violence shelters and 55 percent are denied court orders against abusive partners.

There is another manifestation of family violence that disproportionately affects LGBTQ youth: unsupportive or abusive parents. A June 2010 report by the Center for American progress found that, although 5–10 percent of the youth population in the United States identifies as LGBTQ, LGBTQ teenagers make up 20–40 percent of the homeless youth population. The National Coalition for the Homeless notes that "severe family conflict" is the primary reason for homelessness among LGBTQ youth and that "58.7% of LGBT homeless youth have been sexually victimized compared to 33.4% of heterosexual homeless youth."

In 2013, the U.S. Congress passed the Violence Against Women Reauthorization Act with LGBTQ-inclusive language. This reauthorization guaranteed better access to critical services for LGBTQ victims of domestic violence. Being open to hear all victims' stories is important to ending family violence.

WHO CAN BE AN ABUSER?

Most people believe that family violence only occurs at the hands of men. Statistically speaking, it is true that men commit the majority of acts of violence against family members. But it is a myth that women cannot be abusers. In the data collected by the FBI's National Incident-Based Reporting System (NIBRS) in

Light teasing and roughhousing between siblings is normal, but repeated violence or constant bullying is a form of abuse. Speak to a parent, teacher, or guidance counselor if an older sibling beats you up.

2012, women accounted for approximately one-third of offenders in all reported domestic violence cases. Just as a man can be physically violent with his children or partner, a woman can, too. The popular rapper Eminem became an outspoken critic about abuse at the hands of his mother and often addressed these issues in his music and interviews. The 2009 Academy Award–winning film *Precious* was a popular representation of a family in which the mother was an abuser as well.

And just as abuse can be at the hands of parents, siblings can also be abusers. Older siblings who behave in ways that are physically, emotionally, or sexually abusive may think they are treating their little brothers and sisters in a normal way or

Almost all parents argue at some point or another, but if these arguments become cruel, overly hurtful, or physically violent, then they may constitute abuse.

just teasing them. Many adults laugh about how their older brothers or sisters used to "beat them up all the time." A little good-natured ribbing or playful wrestling is one thing, but serious physical force or bullying used against a sibling is nothing to laugh about. Sexual abuse at the hands of siblings is another form of abuse that is too often overlooked.

Finally, parents may abuse each other. All parents disagree or argue sometimes. This is absolutely normal. Frequently, parents get angry and say things they don't really mean. They might try to say something hurtful when they argue. But when one parent is violent with the other parent, or uses cruel or insulting language, then he or she crosses the line between communicating and verbal or physical abuse. Behavior like this is very difficult for children to see and hear. Children may think that they are to blame for the abuse, but this is never true.

The first step to stopping abuse is understanding what defines family violence. If you are being abused, or know someone who is, there is hope. It is important to learn how to cope, what to do to stop abuse, and how to find the road to peace and recovery.

CHAPTER TWO

WHY DOES IT HAPPEN?

A common response felt by young people who are being abused or witnessing abuse in their families is to wonder how something so awful could be happening. They have no idea why someone they love could be so violent. They may try to justify or ignore the abuse.

Victims of violence and other types of abuse often blame themselves. They convince themselves that they must have done something wrong and deserve to be abused. However, it is extremely important to realize that no one deserves to be abused, ever. But you may be wondering, "If no one deserves it, then why does it happen?"

CAUSES OF FAMILY VIOLENCE

There are many factors that contribute to violence within families. The following scenario shows us some of the leading causes.

Bryan was practicing the piano in his living room. He practiced at least three hours a day because if he didn't hit the notes just right, his father would get angry again.

Bryan didn't really like the piano, but his parents had been pushing him to play since he was little.

Just as Bryan finished playing a composition, his father drunkenly stumbled into the living room. He grabbed Bryan and pulled him up from his bench.

"What's wrong with you, boy?" he shouted, smacking Bryan across the face. The blow was so hard that Bryan fell backward onto the floor. He lay on the ground and trembled. "You'll never be good enough at the piano! You're totally worthless!" shouted Bryan's dad.

"I'm practicing," said Bryan.

His father sighed and said, "My parents couldn't even afford a piano. I just want you to realize how lucky you are. Your mother and I are giving you opportunities we never had and you're wasting them!"

Bryan wished his father would just let him do the things he wanted to, like reading and playing baseball.

Suddenly Bryan's mother walked into the house. She yelled, "Leave him alone!"

Bryan's father looked at her. "Get away from me, you cow!" he screamed at her. "I had a rough day at work."

His mom continued to yell at Bryan's father. "Just because your father hit you when you were a kid doesn't give you the right to hit our son!"

Bryan's dad shouted that he was doing it for Bryan's own good. "I learned a lot about respect from the back of my father's hand!"

DRUG AND ALCOHOL ABUSE

In Bryan's story, many of the causes of violence in families become clear. One of those causes may be drug and alcohol

Drug and alcohol abuse is a common factor in violent situations at home. Parents, siblings, or other relatives who abuse drugs and alcohol are more likely to become physically or verbally violent.

abuse. Bryan's father was drunk when he hit Bryan. Drugs and alcohol affect people's moods, and they can make a bad mood much worse. People under the influence of drugs or alcohol often do not realize what they are doing. They are not in control, and they are much more likely to become abusive.

Parents are not the only ones who abuse drugs and alcohol. Younger siblings may also have to endure abuse at the hands of an older sibling who drinks alcohol or uses recreational drugs. In these cases, the younger children may not feel safe or like their own parents can protect them.

MAJOR STRESS

Bryan's father was also stressed out. He mentioned having had a rough day at work. He took out his frustration on Bryan. This isn't fair. Know that everyone has to deal with stressful situations and must find healthy ways to work through them. Often people who are stressed out try to relieve a lot of the pressure they are feeling by exercising, meditating, reading, riding a bike, talking to a friend, or watching a movie. Many fun activities can help relieve pressure and stress. Physical violence toward other family members is not an acceptable solution.

HIGH EXPECTATIONS

Many times, parents want their children to achieve goals that they never could or to have things they couldn't afford when they were younger. While it is natural and even a great thing for parents to want their children to have opportunities, there is a fine line between motivating a child and pushing too hard.

In our scenario, Bryan's father never had the chance to play an instrument when he was younger. Because of this, he tried to live out his dream through his son. Bryan should have been allowed to pursue his own dreams and to enjoy the activities that he liked.

Bryan's father also wanted him to be perfect. His father got angry with him for not practicing enough or hitting a wrong key. But nobody is perfect. Everybody makes mistakes. Bryan's father expected too much.

FAMILY HISTORY

It is important for adults with a family history of abuse to work through these issues with a therapist. If they do not, some studies suggest they are more likely to resort to abuse themselves.

Finally, and most importantly, Bryan's father had been abused as a child himself. Statistics have shown that, particularly among men, there is a correlation, or link, between victims of abuse becoming adult abusers. Abuse is a cycle that repeats itself. When children are abused, they may eventually abuse their own children, who may then abuse their children, and so on—creating the cycle.

It is important for people who have been abused by members of their families to get help in dealing with their emotions, so that they do not go on to abuse others or suffer from other emotional trauma. They can get this help from a mental health professional, such as a psychiatrist or psychologist. These are doctors who are trained in helping people work through their problems.

BREAKING THE CYCLE OF VIOLENCE

There is a popular belief that all victims of childhood abuse are more likely to become abusers when they grow up. This concept—part of the so-called cycle of violence—simply isn't true. While research does show that individuals with a history of abuse are at an increased risk of committing abuse against their spouses or children, the link is not definitive, and a variety of complex factors play into the continuation of violence. In a 2007 report titled "The Cycle of Violence," compiled and released by the World Health Organization (WHO), the conclusions stated that "only a minority of parents with a history of childhood abuse go on to abuse their own children." Research cited in the report showed that "1 in 6 maltreated boys and girls go on to become violent offenders."

More significantly, the report noted several key factors that research showed help prevent this cycle. Early recognition of abuse was the most important element. Other key elements included:

- Incentives to motivate victims of abuse to finish schooling.
- Proper education on sexual health, parenthood, and the risks of abuse.
- Adequate support and therapy for formerly abused teenagers.

If you currently are or ever were a victim of abuse, know that the cycle can end with you. Ask for the help you need and deserve, and don't feel fated to become an abuser.

ABUSE IS NEVER THE VICTIM'S FAULT

Problems such as eating disorders, depression, and anxiety in children often stem from abusive statements by family members about a child's weight, intelligence, or skills. Victims must understand that they are never responsible for the abuse they suffer.

Bryan felt like a failure because he didn't want to be a maestro on the piano. He thought it was okay for his father to abuse him because he had let his father down by being such a bad player. He also thought that if he liked the piano more, his parents wouldn't fight as much. There was a lot of pressure weighing down on Bryan.

Bryan should not have blamed himself for the abuse. The abuse in Bryan's family was caused by his father's unhappiness. It is up to his father to find ways to cope without resorting to violence. He needs to find safe outlets for his feelings of anger and frustration.

If you are being abused, it is very important for you to understand that this treatment has nothing to do with anything you have done. This is a very difficult thing to accept, but it is true. Abuse stems from the abuser and his or her own problems. If a family member calls you a loser, he or she is probably feeling like a loser. If a parent or other relative is trying to control you, it is probably because he or she cannot control his or her own life.

Understanding that abuse is not your fault is an important part of coping with being abused. It can help you to keep from taking insults too personally. The abuse will still hurt, both physically and emotionally, but understanding the real reasons that it happens will help you build up strength against it.

BUILDING SELF-ESTEEM

Abuse at home can do major damage to an individual's self-esteem. Self-esteem is the feelings a person has about his or her own worth. Abuse can make victims dislike themselves and even want to hurt themselves.

There are ways to fight this feeling. One is called positive self-talk. It involves paying compliments to oneself. For example, when you get up in the morning and brush your teeth, while looking into the mirror, stop and smile. Then say, "You are a beautiful person." Repeat it several times. Then, while you are walking to school, quietly reassure yourself, "I am smart, and I can do anything I want to." You get the idea. This may sound silly, but it really helps.

Positive self-talk is a powerful tool to counteract the negative things others may say about you. For example, if your mother or older sibling always tells you that you are ugly, tell yourself that you are attractive. If an aunt or uncle calls

Positive self-talk can help victims of emotional abuse regain their confidence. Look at yourself in the mirror and give yourself compliments before school each morning. Remind yourself that you are handsome or beautiful.

you useless, tell yourself you are valuable. Remind yourself of your good qualities. Even if you do not believe the words you are saying, keep saying them. Your mind will be talked into believing them, and whatever you believe about yourself is what you become.

Coping with abuse and understanding why it happens are important first steps, but the next step is to find ways to make the abuse stop.

CHAPTER THREE

STEPS TO STOP VIOLENCE AT HOME

F amily members suffering from abuse usually feel helpless and at the mercy of the abuser. They think that there is nothing they can do to make things better. Often, they will try to pretend the abuse is not happening. Sometimes people think that if they ignore something bad it will go away, but violence in families does not work this way. The abuse just continues on—sometimes for many years—because nobody ever does anything to stop it.

SPEAK UP!

The best way to stop family violence is to tell somebody about it. Speak up! Talk to somebody outside your family—a teacher, a guidance counselor, a coach, the police, a priest, an imam, or a rabbi—about what is

A great first step to stopping an abusive situation in your family is to tell a trusted adult outside the family, such as a teacher, a coach, or a religious authority. He or she can help you take the right steps to end violence in your home.

25

happening. Any adult you trust should be able to help in some way, even if he or she simply suggests the name of someone else to whom you should talk.

There are also places where you can go to get away from someone who is hurting you. Domestic violence shelters are safe, comfortable places where victims of family violence can stay. The people who work at the shelter will be able to advise you on the next steps that need to be taken. You can also find valuable information by contacting domestic violence organizations and hotlines. Several domestic violence organizations have tips on their websites to help victims of family violence reach out without being caught by their abusers. It is very important to talk to someone else because it is extremely difficult to stop family violence by yourself.

APP ASSISTANCE: NEW WAYS TO REPORT ABUSE

With developments in technology have come new and improved ways to support victims of family violence. One such development is the smartphone and tablet app Aspire News. This clever app was developed by When Georgia Smiled: The Robin McGraw Revelation Foundation, an organization dedicated to supporting victims of domestic violence and sexual assault.

Disguised as a standard news app with fake reports filling the front page, the app allows users to access local domestic violence resources, set emergency contacts, and—with a triple tap on the screen—alert their chosen contacts as well as local authorities and emergency services providers in a potentially violent situation. Because victims of domestic abuse often have their phones or computers monitored at home, the disguised home page allows these victims to keep a lifesaving resource on hand, one that can allow them to alert authorities without tipping off their aggressors.

Apps such as Aspire News are the future of reporting abuse. In May 2015, a Florida woman named Cheryl Treadway cleverly used a pizza delivery app to report an abusive situation in which her boyfriend was holding both her and her three children hostage. The man would not let Treadway use her phone until she convinced him to let her order a pizza via a pizza delivery app. In the comments section of her order, the victim wrote, "Please help. Get 911 to me." Under the toppings for her pizza, Treadway again listed "911 hostage help!" Her quick thinking and clever app use got police to the house without alerting her aggressor and potentially provoking more violence.

Other helpful apps such as iMatter provide counseling and resources for recovering victims of abuse. In 2011, the U.S. Department of Health and Human Services and the White House Office of Science and Technology Policy collaborated to challenge app developers to work on new apps that would empower young adults to prevent abuse and violence.

STEPS TO AVOID

Fighting back against an abuser is generally not a good idea. Resorting to violence could put a victim in an even more dangerous situation, provoking greater anger from the aggressor. Never pull out a weapon, such as a gun or a knife, to try to keep an abuser away from you. He or she may try to take the weapon and use it against you, or you could end up accidentally hurting yourself or another family member. Weapons are especially dangerous when drugs or alcohol are involved. People who are drunk or high are more likely to use a weapon and less likely to be careful with it.

Running away without a destination is another bad idea. Where would you sleep? How would you get money to eat and clothe yourself? What if it gets cold? Living on the streets is dangerous and often deadly. Unfortunately, this is what happens to many young victims of family violence. They want to get away from the abuse so badly that they just leave their homes without knowing where they will go. These young people may end up hurt, killed, or permanently homeless. Homeless teens often end up dealing drugs or prostituting their bodies in order to get by. Do not let this happen to you! If you feel you must leave your home, call a domestic abuse shelter first.

ABUSE IS ILLEGAL

It may be difficult to believe, but until the mid-19th century, most countries' legal systems allowed men to abuse their wives and children. Laws ignored violence in families and believed it was an important part of a husband's authority over his family. The police considered all disputes between family members "private" and, therefore, would not get involved.

This started to change in the late 1800s. In 1850, Tennessee became the first state to make "wife beating" illegal. By 1920, violence against spouses became illegal throughout the United States. In the 1970s, public awareness for domestic violence against women increased, and, in the 1990s, awareness grew for domestic violence against men, as well.

Today, all forms of family violence are against the law throughout North America. Someone who abuses members of his or her family can be arrested. The government has also become involved, creating organizations to keep track of and to raise awareness about domestic abuse.

Always remember that family violence is illegal. The law stands firmly on the side of the victims of family violence, and government agencies and other organizations will work to protect these victims.

WHY SOME FAMILIES DON'T SEEK HELP

People who have never lived in a household where there is family violence often ask themselves why a victim would not try to get help. They wonder, "Why would any human being just keep being abused, over and over again, and never do anything about it?"

Family members are often afraid of the consequences of reporting abuse, but the law can help protect them. Victims of abuse can use an attorney to help secure their property and protect their safety from former abusers.

Fear is probably the biggest reason. Victims are constantly afraid of what an abuser might do to them if they report their abuse to anybody. This is why domestic violence shelters, emergency hotlines, and apps that help victims report their abuse without detection by their abusers are so important. Shelters, in particular, can protect victims from further abuse and help keep them out of a violent situation.

When a family member is abused by another family member, relationships and emotions are very confusing. On the one hand, you love your parent, sibling, or other relative, but on the other hand, you hate this person for hurting you. It can become very complicated to balance these two feelings. Because of this, victims often hold back from getting help, because they do not want someone they love to be arrested. They may think that they can change the abuser on their own. But if they really love the abuser, they should realize that stopping the violence and getting help is the best thing they could do for that person.

Low self-esteem can also keep victims from speaking out. They may really believe that it is okay for a family member to hit them and insult them. They might feel ugly, stupid, or useless and that they deserve to be treated badly. These feelings take away their strength. People who do not believe in themselves are not likely to stand up for themselves. They also might believe that an abusive relationship is better than no relationship at all.

Families who suffer from abuse without getting help have to work very hard to keep their situations a secret. Parents may put makeup on their children's bruises. Children willfully or sometimes are forced to

Because of confusing emotions or fear, many victims prefer to cover up domestic violence and avoid reporting abusive family members to the police. However, this will only let violence continue at home.

invent stories to explain why they have broken bones or deep cuts. Battered wives may take to wearing long pants or skirts to make sure that bruising won't show.

But suffering families do not just hide their scars from the outside world. Oftentimes they hide them from each other as well. Family members might never mention abuse to one another. Everybody knows that it is happening, but nobody talks about it.

Family members are frequently afraid to discuss or think about what is happening. They know that if they looked closely at the situation, they would have to face up to the problem. They would have to do something they probably wouldn't be prepared to do—seek help. But if that first step is not taken, they could end up living their entire lives in pain and fear.

CHAPTER FOUR

OVERCOMING FAMILY VIOLENCE

Family violence leaves scars—both physical and emotional. In a family where one person has treated the other members in a violent way, the abuser must recognize the problem and do something about it in order to change the situation. Just saying he or she will try to change is not enough. He or she must seek professional help. The problems that cause family violence cannot be solved alone.

DECIDING TO LEAVE

One of the hardest things for victims of family violence is to decide to leave their homes. It is important to have a safe contact or plan for where to initially go. Consider the following scenario.

My mom and I finally did it. We got away from my dad. He was in a rage last night, throwing us around and breaking things. I think he was on drugs. My dad's been addicted to cocaine for as long as I can remember, but he thinks I don't know about it.

My mom grabbed me, and we went out to the car. He followed us, shouting. We got in and locked the doors.

Often, victims of family violence must leave quickly while their abuser is asleep or not home. Having a secure place to go, such as another relative's or close friend's house, is the first step to safety. Reporting the violence must follow.

He tried to jump on the hood of the car, but he fell off. My mom backed out of the driveway, and the next thing I knew we were at my uncle Eddie's house. I couldn't believe it was happening.

We told Uncle Eddie everything. My mom was talking about the beatings and the cocaine through a stream of tears. My uncle was angry with my father and concerned about us. He said he would take care of us until we worked out our plans. He made up beds for us and made sure the house was locked up and secure.

Today, my dad called. My mom and I both got on the phone together.

"I'm sorry, you guys. Come home. I'll never do that again, I swear," he cried. "I've learned my lesson."

My mother said, "You've said that before. I don't believe you anymore."

I could hear my dad sniffling and weeping. My mother seemed sad, but she did not give in. She told him that maybe someday we could be a family again, but he had to get help first. She told him he had to go into a rehab program and see a therapist to help him work through his issues.

"Oh, come on!" he said. "I don't have a drug problem! And I don't need to see a shrink! I'm not crazy!"

My mom sighed. "Until you face the facts, we cannot live together in peace." She hung up the phone and cried, but I knew she made the right decision for us.

Victims of abuse have many challenges to face after seeking help or getting away from their abuser. How do you know when or if the abuser has truly changed? If the abuser supplied some or all of the money for the household, how will you support yourselves now? If you have gone to a shelter or to live with another relative, will you have to give up your home? In the case of married partners, should you file for divorce or wait to see how things work out? What are your rights?

These are not easy questions to answer. Victims of family violence must search deep inside themselves to decide what is best for their families. Often a victim will feel lost without the abuser and run right back to him or her at the first sign of an apology. This is a mistake. No matter how sorry abusers seem, no matter how much they cry and beg, going back just opens

COUNT ON SUPPORT!
CRUNCHING NUMBERS ON
DOMESTIC VIOLENCE PROGRAMS

It can be very difficult to get accurate statistics to show just how widespread family violence is. One of the primary reasons for this is that many victims of domestic abuse and family violence do not or cannot safely report their abuse. Another reason it can be difficult to collect accurate data on the prevalence of family violence is that many of the domestic violence programs do not record identity-specific information on the people who seek their services. This is essential for preserving the anonymity and safety of victims of family violence. So how can we calculate the benefits of domestic violence prevention programs?

Each year, the National Network to End Domestic Violence (NNEDV) conducts a one-day census on adults and children who seek domestic violence service nationwide. In one twenty-four-hour period, the NNEDV counts each individual who seeks some form of services from participating domestic violence programs (1,649 of the 1,905 identified domestic violence programs in the United States) and the success rate of meeting these victims' needs. On September 17, 2013, 19,431 children and 16,917 adults found refuge in domestic violence shelters or transitional housing. Another 30,233 adults

(continued on the next page)

(continued from the previous page)

and children sought nonresidential services such as counseling or legal advocacy. In the same twenty-four-hour period, 20,267 hotlines calls were answered and 23,389 individuals attended training sessions in violence education and prevention.

Unfortunately, the NNEDV 2013 census also registered 9,641 unmet requests for services, 60 percent of which were for housing needs. Unable to get help, these victims often return to their abusers or become homeless. Increased funding and public awareness are important keys to expanding domestic violence programs to help more victims. Consider starting a school campaign to raise funding or collecting unused, old cell phones in a phone drive to benefit these programs. Find more information from the NNEDV's website (http://nnedv.org/).

the door for more pain. It is only a matter of time before the violence begins again. Abusers must seek professional help to get to the root of their problems.

MOVING ON

Once a family puts a stop to the abuse, and the victims of abuse are safe, what then? If you are a victim of abuse, one of the most helpful things to realize is that you are not alone. Many other people are dealing with the same feelings and experiences that you are.

Talking with a counselor or other therapist often helps victims of family violence understand what happened to them and move beyond their pasts. Domestic violence shelters and schools generally offer guidance services to young people who seek them.

One thing that is certain in this situation is that the entire family will need professional help in order to recover. Therapy is an important part of recovery.

What is therapy? There are many different types of therapy, but the main purpose of therapy is to help people heal themselves by learning how to deal with their feelings. Therapy can open people's minds, and teach them things about themselves and their lives that they have never realized.

One type of therapy happens between an abuse survivor and a professional psychologist or psychiatrist. Survivors meet with their chosen counselor and talk about things that have happened to them. They discuss their feelings and try to plan out what their next steps should be.

Many survivors have great success with this kind of therapy. Other people may prefer therapy in groups. In this kind of therapy, a certified therapist leads a small group of people with a common problem (such as family violence) in discussing their feelings together. They share their experiences, offer suggestions and support, and help each other to get through tough times. Some people prefer this to one-on-one therapy because it gives the victims multiple perspectives and a variety of advice on personal issues. Positive interaction with others who share your pain is an important part of recovery from any painful experience.

It may be hard to accept, but recovery does not happen overnight. It may take years to heal from the emotional trauma of abuse. However, with therapy, patience, and time, many victims are able to move beyond their violent family situation, put a permanent stop to the cycle of abuse, and live a happy, fulfilling life.

GLOSSARY

abuse Intentional harm toward someone in a physical or emotional way.

anonymity The condition of being unknown to others or remaining anonymous.

battered Physically abused; this term is used most often to describe an abused wife.

correlation A mutual relation or link between two different variables.

discipline To punish in a caring way; discipline is intended to help someone grow, not to hurt him or her.

domestic violence shelter Safe place where victims of family violence live temporarily.

emotional abuse Act of intentionally damaging someone's self-esteem using words.

fated Predestined; subject to or guided by fate.

maestro An important composer or conductor of music.

neglect Act of intentionally withholding something needed by a family member such as food, clothing, shelter, or love.

prevalence The condition of being widespread or common.

psychiatrist Doctor trained to help people deal with their feelings and problems.

psychologist Professional counselor trained to help people deal with their feelings and problems.

self-esteem Good feelings people have about themselves and their bodies.

sexual abuse Sexual touching of someone who does not want to be touched.

therapy Speaking with a psychiatrist, psychologist, counselor, or group of people to help deal with feelings and overcome problems.

FOR MORE INFORMATION

Please note: If you are in immediate danger, dial 911.

Centre for Research on Children and Families (CRCF)
Suite 106, Wilson Hall
3506 University Street,
Montréal, QC H3A 2A7
Canada
(514) 398-7068
Website: http://www.mcgill.ca/crcf
The McGill CRCF is an academic center dedicated to cutting-
edge research and program development for the welfare of
children and families. It seeks to improve child welfare through
improved government policy and community building.

Canadian Women's Foundation
133 Richmond St. West, Suite 504
Toronto, ON M5H 2L3
Canada
(866) 293-4483
Website: http://www.canadianwomen.org
Launched in 1991, the Canadian Women's Foundation seeks to
improve and rights for women and girls throughout Canada.
It has raised over forty million dollars and supported over
1,200 community programs since its founding.

Center Against Domestic Violence (CADV)
25 Chapel Street, Suite 904
Brooklyn, NY 11201
(718) 254-9134
Website: http://www.cadvny.org
The CADV provides support, resources, and education for victims and survivors of domestic violence.

Elder Abuse Toronto
2 Billingham Road, Suite 306
Toronto, ON M9B 6E1
Canada
(416) 916-6728
Website: http://www.elderabuseontario.com
Elder Abuse Toronto focuses on training, policy, and public
education in the field of elder care to protect senior citizens
from abuse and to give them a voice.

National Coalition Against Domestic Violence (NCADV)
1 Broadway, Suite B210
Denver, CO 80203
(303) 839-1852
Website: http://www.ncadv.org
Since 1978, the NCADV has worked to raise awareness of
domestic violence, support its victims, and change public
policy to these same ends.

National Network to End Domestic Violence (NNEDV)
1400 16th Street NW, Suite 330
Washington, DC 20036
(202) 543-5566
Website: http://nnedv.org
The NNEDV is the premier organization working to give a voice
to victims of domestic violence and create political and social
changes that will end violence against women.

The Network/La Red
P.O. Box 6011
Boston, MA 02114
Phone: (617) 695-0877

Hotline: (617) 742-4911

Website: http://tnlr.org

The Network/La Red is a bilingual, English/Spanish organization led by survivors to end family violence and provide support to victims of partner abuse in LGBTQ communities. It does this by providing public education and support services.

Su Casa

3840 Woodruff Ave., Suite 203

Long Beach, CA 90808

Phone: (562) 421-6537

24-Hour Hotline: (562) 402-4888

Website: http://www.sucasadv.org

Founded in 1979, Su Casa is dedicated to raising community awareness of domestic violence. It operates shelters (which provide certified early childhood education) and transitional housing for families escaping abuse.

WEBSITES

Because of the changing nature of Internet links, Rosen Publishing has developed an online list of websites related to the subject of this book. This site is updated regularly. Please use this link to access the list:

http://www.rosenlinks.com/FIY/Viol

FOR FURTHER READING

Bryfonski, Dedria, ed. *Family Violence* (Current Controversies). Detroit, MI: Greenhaven Press, 2013.

Cupala, Holly. *Don't Breathe a Word*. New York, NY: HarperTeen, 2011.

Floric, Marylee & Matthew Broyles. *Sexual Abuse* (Girls' Health). New York, NY: Rosen Central, 2012.

Gerdes, Louise I., ed. *Domestic Violence* (Opposing Viewpoints). Detroit, MI: Greenhaven Press, 2012.

Halbrook, Kristin. *Nobody But Us*. New York, NY: HarperTeen, 2013.

Henningfeld, Diane Andrews, ed. *Family Violence* (Global Viewpoints). Detroit, MI: Greenhaven Press, 2012.

Kenney, Karen Latchana. *Domestic Violence* (Essential Issues). Edina, MN: ABDO Publishing, 2012.

LaBella, Laura. *Living in a Violent Household*. New York, NY: Rosen Publishing, 2016.

Langan, John. *Search for Safety*. New York, NY: Scholastic, 2012.

Larson, Karl, Heath Dingwell, William McCay & Robert N. Golden. *The Truth about Violence*. New York, NY: Facts On File, 2011.

Michaels, Vanessa Lynn & Jeremy Harrow. *Frequently Asked Questions about Family Violence*. New York, NY: Rosen Publishing, 2012.

Miles, Liz. *Coping with Domestic Violence*. Oxford, U.K.: Raintree, 2012.

Morgan, Lori & Kathy R. Kaulbacj. *Healing the Bruises*. Halifax, NS: Formac Publishing Company, 2013.

Newton, Sydney & Julie Gerrits. *Child Abuse*. New York, NY: Crabtree Publishing Company, 2011.

Stewart, Sheila & Rae Simons. *When Daddy Hit Mommy*. Broomall, PA: Mason Crest Publishers, 2011.

INDEX

ABOUT THE AUTHORS

Delilah Banks is a writer and educator living in Hoboken, New Jersey. She has a passion for teaching and making sure her students can always count on her classroom to be a safe environment.

John Giacobello is a writer and musician living in New York City.

PHOTO CREDITS

Designer: Michael Moy; Editor: Jacob Steinberg;
Photo Researcher: Nicole Baker